Original title:
The Forest's Fabric

Copyright © 2025 Creative Arts Management OÜ
All rights reserved.

Author: Victor Mercer
ISBN HARDBACK: 978-1-80567-071-1
ISBN PAPERBACK: 978-1-80567-151-0

Barkbound Narratives

In trees with faces, they tell a joke,
A squirrel's tail waves, a hat made of oak.
Beneath leafy whispers, giggles abide,
As mushrooms dance, in their colorful stride.

Logs lie in wait, for a story to spring,
A woodpecker's tap is a rhythm to sing.
With branches that wiggle, and roots that sway,
Nature's cartoony playtime at bay.

Hemming the Celestial Canopy

The stars drop by for a pajama feast,
With firefly lanterns, they party at least!
The moon in pajamas, very silly but fine,
While night critters gather to sip some moonshine.

A comet's a guest, bringing laughter profound,
As squirrels pass cakes, and the owls look around.
Everything twinkles, the backdrop's divine,
In stitches and seams, the heavens align.

Nature's Handcrafted Harmonies

A concert of chirps, each bird takes a turn,
With leaves as the audience, they giggle and churn.
Raccoons clap paws, while the fox pulls a face,
As ants conduct tiny, a bustling embrace.

The wind strums a tune, on branches that sway,
Grasshoppers sing bass, while loons lead the way.
A symphony born from a zany delight,
Beats mixed with laughter, under the moonlight.

Mending the Earth's Canopy

A bear stitches clouds with a needle of sun,
Sewing up patches for everyone's fun.
With humor and thread, the sky gets a grin,
As rabbits bring fabric with a hop and a spin.

The plants wear their colors like clothes on a spree,
As butterflies twirl, feeling fancy and free.
It's a tailor-made scene, in this goofy old patch,
Where nature's the artist, and joy is the catch.

Nature's Silken Veil

In the wood where squirrels play,
A spider's web holds bright display.
The bees wear hats much too oversized,
Buzzing in circles, oh so surprised.

Mushrooms dance in a little parade,
Toadstools twirl, never afraid.
While raccoons in tuxes steal the show,
Sipping acorns, oh what a glow!

Patterns in the Underbrush

Leaves twist and turn, all in a spin,
With squirrels in shades, trying to win.
They gossip about the chipmunk brigade,
In the gossiping roots, we serenade.

A fox in sneakers dashes on by,
While owls hoot lyrics from on high.
The grasshoppers jump in their new ballet,
It's a quirky dance, hip hip hooray!

The Weft of Wooded Dreams

An acorn cap, a jaunty hat,
On a pinecone, the cat sat flat.
As fairies giggle and weep with glee,
They sprinkle magic like confetti.

Bugs gather 'round for a karaoke night,
A cricket's voice cut through with might.
The trees sway gently, they cannot resist,
To join the fun in a leafy twist!

Stitches Among the Trees

In tree trunks, whispers tell tales of yore,
Of beavers that build and then build some more.
While hedgehogs plan their next big affair,
With hedges as bouncers, watch out for hair!

A ferret in boots skates past the brook,
With a raccoon chef cooking by the nook.
The woodland's laughter, a delightful tease,
In the stitches of life, we do as we please!

A Patchwork of Pine and Fern

In a realm where squirrels wear shoes,
And raccoons have dance parties too.
The pines gossip with cheeky ferns,
While nature spins in silly turns.

The mushrooms wear hats made of dew,
And caterpillars sip on brew.
A tapestry woven with laughter's thread,
In this patch where the wild things tread.

Twisted Tales of Twigs

There once was a twig with a twisty grin,
Who claimed he could dance on a tightrope thin.
Trees told tales of his balancing skills,
As the critters cheered with raucous thrills.

His buddies, the leaves, joined in the fun,
Spinning pirouettes under the sun.
A parade of branches laughed loud and clear,
In this woodland circus, nothing to fear!

The Quilted Wilderness

The ground is a patchwork, soft and bright,
With daisies peeking, what a delight!
Frogs in bow ties croak as they leap,
While rabbits divide their carrots in heaps.

A hedgehog knits with a thimble so grand,
Creating designs only she could have planned.
Her yarn is the grass, her needles the sun,
In this quilted wonder, life's always fun!

Variegated Veins of Verdance

Leaves wear colors that wiggle and sway,
As if they're attending a grand cabaret.
Bamboo flutes whistle a tune so absurd,
While chipmunks form bands, oh, haven't you heard?

With poppies in tutus performing a show,
And daisies in sunglasses, stealing the glow.
In this variegated world where laughter takes flight,
Every day's whimsy is a sheer delight!

Weaving the Winding Paths

In tangled threads, the path does sway,
Squirrels dance in a nutty ballet.
A rabbit hops and gives a wink,
While mushrooms giggle, pink on pink.

Lost in a maze of leafy green,
A deer stuck in a yoga scene.
Birds wear hats made from tree bark,
Chirping tunes, they're quite the lark.

Green Hues and Earthy Tones

Frogs in bow ties croak with glee,
Preparing for the grandest spree.
With polka dots upon their backs,
They play hide and seek with the snazzy tracks.

In every shade, a laugh unfolds,
The sun smiles down, as warmth it holds.
Bouncing beetles roll like balls,
As dandelion fluff gently falls.

The Soft Embrace of Moss

Underfoot, a carpet feels so plush,
Where critters pause, and slowly hush.
A snail in slippers makes a tour,
As mushrooms offer tea—quite sure!

The mossy hugs are sweet and light,
As sleepy owls blink through the night.
With sleepy laughter from all around,
Their giggles soften without a sound.

Secrets Entwined in Foliage

Whispers travel through leafy hides,
As chipmunks plot their snack-filled rides.
They conspire with the winds that peek,
Stealing crumbs from a hiker's cheek.

A secret grove of giggly trees,
Swaying with the buzzing bees.
Hiding treasures beneath the bark,
In this place, the dreams embark.

Textiles of the Whispering Pines

In the woods where squirrels scheme,
A tailor's shop awaits, it seems.
With acorn caps and mushroom hats,
They stitch and sew, like chatty bats.

Spiders spin their webs so fine,
They call it art, a true design.
But when the wind starts to play,
The whole thing blows clean away!

Fiber of the Hidden Vale

In shadows deep, the critters prance,
The rabbits start a dance-off chance.
With dandelion fluff for shirts,
They hop around in goofy spurts.

The foxes weave their leafy tales,
While sharing jokes of lost trails.
With every twist and playful jibe,
Their laughter echoes in the tribe.

Silken Threads of Sunlight

Beams of light like threads so bright,
Stitch the day with pure delight.
The sunbeams tickle up the trees,
While birds in shades of red and glee.

A wren in fashion made of gold,
Struts around, so bold, so bold!
And when a ray's forgotten spot,
A squirrel's wig becomes the plot!

The Lattice of Life Unseen

Underneath the leafy guise,
The ants are crafting funky ties.
With bits of leaf and drops of dew,
They cover worlds in colors new.

A beetle's got a plaid design,
While ladybugs sip grape divine.
And when the moon starts to rise high,
They twirl their threads, oh me, oh my!

Shadows in the Green Embrace

In the woods where squirrels chatter,
A raccoon wears a hat, oh what a matter!
The trees gossip in breezy tones,
While rabbits dance on hidden stones.

A deer gives a bow, so polite and neat,
While owls try to keep time with their beat.
The sun peeks down, a playful spark,
As the shadows play tag till it's dark.

The Sylvan Quilt

Leaves fall like confetti, a jumble of hues,
Each patch tells a tale, in reds and blues.
Woodpeckers tap out their humor on bark,
While a fox tells a joke, brightening the dark.

Mushrooms in circles, a dance of delight,
Frogs sing their ballads beneath the moonlight.
In cozy corners where shadows reside,
Laughter of crickets, the woodland's pride.

Patterns of the Woodland Heart

Twigs twist and turn in a curious trance,
While a badger steps forward, ready to dance.
The flowers gossip, sharing their thoughts,
As butterflies giggle, their colors in knots.

A chipmunk juggles acorns with flair,
While a wise old owl gives them all a stare.
The sun paints the ground with a playful grin,
As nature's madcap chaos begins to spin.

Nature's Interwoven Symphony

In the glades where laughter echoes all day,
A toad sings opera, what a curious play!
The breeze is a conductor, gentle and spry,
While the branches nod along, oh my, oh my!

Squirrels debate on the best summer snack,
While hedgehogs giggle from their cozy pack.
With fireflies twinkling like stars in the gloom,
The woodland hums softly, a comedic tune.

Cradle of the Green Canopy

In the branches, squirrels dance,
Hitching rides on breezes' prance.
Bumblebees buzz with wiggly glee,
While ants argue, 'Who has the best tea?'

Mushrooms wear hats, oh so bright,
With tiny bugs hosting tea every night.
A raccoon juggles acorns and nuts,
Chasing his tail, oh what silly struts!

Under the shade, a lizard twirls,
While nearby, a rabbit gives silly whirls.
Frogs croak songs that sound quite grand,
As the whole woods join in a marching band.

Leaves giggle as they tumble down,
Whispers of secrets in a leafy gown.
Nature's laughter echoes wide,
In this cradle where whimsies abide.

Braids of Twigs and Dreams

Twigs are woven, snug and neat,
In a cozy home for woodland feet.
A raccoon runs a little inn,
With berries served, he never lets in kin.

Dancing fireflies spark the night,
With glow-in-the-dark fashion, oh what a sight!
A wise old owl offers his two cents,
To cranky bats and their noisy pretense.

A fox in spectacles reads on a log,
While critters gather 'round, misty and fog.
Nachos made from nuts and bark,
Filling the woods with a cheerful spark.

The brush is abuzz with laughter and cheer,
As friends come together, spreading good beer.
In a place where dreams take flight,
Braids of joy spin wild in the moonlight.

Nature's Woven Chronicles

Tales unfold among the trees,
Squirrels whispering secrets with ease.
Every leaf has a story to tell,
About deer that dance or beavers that fell.

A badger plays chess with a wise old crow,
While hedgehogs gossip and giggle, 'Whoa!'
A mushroom wants to be a big star,
But only glows softly—oh how bizarre!

Rabbits plot a carrot heist,
While birds critique their lunch on a feast.
The wind tells jokes, all puns and spins,
As laughter erupts where the fun begins.

In this tapestry where tales entwine,
Each creature's journey a gentle sign.
Woven laughter through branches sways,
In this merry woodland, where whimsy stays.

Stitches of the Sylvan Soul

Patchwork leaves in colors bright,
Quilting the woods with pure delight.
A porcupine with prickly flair,
Throws a party for those who dare.

Beetles rap on fallen trunks,
While shy foxes croon over funky punks.
Nature knits blankets of sunlit threads,
For napping rabbits in their garden beds.

Singing streams carry melodies clear,
As playful otters paddle near,
A skunk struts by, with a boisterous tune,
Under a borrowed hat from the moon.

So gather 'round, dear friends and foes,
In this crafty world where nonsense grows.
With stitches of laughter and joy combined,
We weave a wild tale for the sweetly inclined.

Interwoven Journeys Through Shadow

In tangled paths, we dance around,
With squirrels gossiping, making sound.
The trees sway like they hold a party,
While mushrooms plot to get quite hearty.

Beneath the boughs, we stumble and trip,
And giggle at toadstools, doing a flip.
A rabbit mocks with a cheeky grin,
As twigs and leaves get into a spin.

Unruly branches play hide and seek,
Tickling our senses, making us squeak.
The shadows chuckle, a tickling breeze,
While we chase giggles among the trees.

In this jolly maze, let laughter reign,
Where every twist brings joy, not pain.
For in this jungle of quirky sights,
We find our joy in nature's delights.

Branches Softly Entwined

With branches chatting, gossip flies,
About the squirrel's latest tries.
One acorn drops, a slapstick show,
While owls pretend they don't quite know.

Beneath the shade where shadows creep,
The ferns conduct a dance, so deep.
With every step, a crunching sound,
Nature's laughter all around.

A busy bee buzzes with zest,
While underfoot, ants never rest.
Two rabbits argue about the best,
Carrots or lettuce? What a jest!

In this embrace of green and brown,
We'll play our part, we won't back down.
With every rustle, and every sway,
The forest laughs; come out and play!

Harmony Beneath the Canopy

From leafy heights, the sun spills cheer,
While critters chirp, and we draw near.
The breeze carries a joke or two,
About a tree that wished it flew.

With branches swaying, whispers start,
Notes of nature playing its part.
A woodpecker drums on a hollow trunk,
Making rhythms like a funky punk.

Beneath this arch of emerald green,
We laugh at the sights, a playful scene.
While ants hold parades all day long,
In a fashion that feels all wrong!

Join in the chorus of nature's glee,
For in this wild, we are carefree.
Among the roots and laughing leaves,
We weave our tales, while mischief cleaves.

Echoes of Growth and Regrowth

As tiny seeds sprout and stretch their toes,
The dance begins with wobbly bows.
A garden of antics, oh what a sight,
As colors clash in a comical fight.

The trees chuckle, their stories old,
In whispers of mischief, so bold.
With every leaf, a giggle flies,
As nature paints with silly dyes.

The mushrooms sprout in curious rows,
One claims it's the best, no one knows.
While winds play tunes only branches hear,
Each note of laughter draws us near.

So here we stand in this lively play,
In sync with nature, come what may.
For in this realm where humor grows,
We find our joy in the funny shows.

Gossamer in the Glen

In a glen where spiders weave,
A web that's slightly hard to believe.
The bugs get caught, oh what a sight,
Dancing in circles, all day and night.

A squirrel, with flair, struts on the line,
Wearing a cape, feeling divine.
He leaps but gets tangled, oh dear me,
A fashion faux pas for all to see.

Bats gossip in shadows, whispering schemes,
While owls pen novels on midnight beams.
A whole lot of wiggles, laughs, and games,
In the glen where everything's slightly insane.

So if you wander to this strange nook,
Bring a good heart and a good book.
For laughter awaits in this whimsical scene,
Where the gossamer glimmers, and all is serene.

The Stitching of Seasons

Winter's a quilter, sewing snowflakes,
Stitching them tight with frosty mistakes.
Spring threads in flowers, colors galore,
Each bloom a surprise on the fabric's floor.

Summer paints in warm yellows and greens,
Slapping on sun like a well-versed dream.
Autumn, with oranges, snips at the seams,
As leaves twirl down, in spirals, it seems.

Yet all get tangled in threads of delight,
A patchwork of giggles in soft twilight.
They laugh as they scramble, a comedic sight,
In this sewing circle, both day and night.

So join in the stitching, it's all in good fun,
Count every giggle beneath the sun.
For every mishap adds flair to the art,
In this bustling tapestry, it's a wild heart.

Interlaced Ironwoods

Two trees debate, 'Is it you or me?
Or are we just branches of one grand spree?'
Ironwoods jibe in their rigid stance,
And sway to the rhythm of their own dance.

A raccoon beneath, holding a grudge,
Scoffs at the trees, says, 'Don't you judge!'
For I've seen you trip on a squirrel's tail,
Now who's the wise one who will prevail?

The trees chuckle deep, a resonant sound,
As bunnies do acrobatics around.
But with every laugh, the roots intertwine,
Linking their jokes like old pals at wine.

Together they fashion a canopy ripe,
In this madcap place, full of type.
It's a circus of joy in a wooded parade,
Where each snap of a twig is a new escapade.

Canvas of Canopy Creatures

A canvas hangs high, stretched tight in the air,
Home to the creatures who don't have a care.
A dogwood tree hosts a party so bold,
Where critters paint stories that never get old.

A woodpecker drums, keeping beat with the sun,
While a gang of raccoons vie for a pun.
Each flick of a tail brings a raucous cheer,
As laughter echoes through the sky, oh dear!

A lineup of ants march with style and grace,
Their tiny parade is a comical race.
They trip on a twig, tumble, and roll,
But up they spring, with humor as their goal.

So come join the fun, under pictures so bright,
In a canvas of chaos, pure delight.
For laughter entwines with each flutter and cheer,
As the creatures celebrate the whimsy here.

Roots Beneath the Surface

Deep below, the roots do creep,
Whispering secrets, never sleep.
They gossip about trees so tall,
And share their thoughts on a squirrel's fall.

One claims a neighbor's bark is fake,
The other laughs, 'That's quite the mistake!'
In this underground chatty spree,
Who knew they'd crack jokes so free?

Voices in the Verdant Weave

In the green tapestry, vines entwine,
A parrot squawks, 'I'm feeling fine!'
A snail responds with a slow quick rhyme,
'You keep moving, I'll bide my time.'

They debate who's more stylish today,
With petals and leaves on ambitious display.
The punchline lands from a frog nearby,
'I'm the fly-catching charm, oh my!'

Interlaced in Evergreen

Evergreen jokes fill the air,
A pine whispers to a cedar, 'Beware!
Don't let the elf paint you a shade,
He thinks he's a master, but I'm not afraid!'

The birch joins in with a cheeky chime,
'At least I'm straight, not twisted with time!'
The laughter echoing through the trees,
As branches bob and sway with ease.

Treading Through the Woven Wild

On a path of laughter, we skip and hop,
Grass tickles toes, oh, we can't stop!
A raccoon peeks with a pie in hand,
'Could this wild feast be perfectly planned?'

A chipmunk shouts, 'There's pie for me too!'
As leaves chuckle and dance in the dew.
Nature's banquet is a sight to see,
Where all the creatures dine with glee!

Plumage and Petals Intertwined

In a grove where birds chat loud,
Petals flutter like a proud crowd.
Feathers tickle the daisies' tops,
As squirrels giggle and do flips and hops.

Bumblebees dance like they're on stage,
While wise old owls turn the page.
A gust blows, and chaos breaks loose,
The blossoms blush, but they're not confused.

Larks in coats of bright and bold,
Share secrets in the leaves of gold.
A rabbit with shades struts by,
Dancing through blooms with a cheeky sigh.

And when dusk falls, the laughs don't cease,
As moonlight whispers, "Dance, sweet piece!"
The petals sway, the feathers sway,
In a gathering that lasts till the day.

Tangle of Trunks and Tales

In a maze where branches bend low,
Trees share their woes and big-time woes.
Each trunk has tales to spin like yarn,
Of squirrels who ate one too many nuts on the lawn.

Barking dogs bet on which tree's best,
While foxes giggle in a leafy nest.
A twisting vine cheers on the fray,
Raccoons toast to another wild day.

Branches dance in the wind's embrace,
While mushrooms giggle, their secret place.
A woodpecker plays the drum so sweet,
And crickets join in with cheerful beat.

At night the roots tell ghostly jokes,
While playful ghouls tease oblivious folks.
A tangle of trunks, a tangle of lore,
Leaves everyone wanting to explore!

Aubergine Alder and Golden Oak

Beneath the boughs of colors so bright,
An aubergine tree tosses sprites of fright.
While golden oaks giggle and sway,
Pretending they're wise, as they're sleeping all day.

A dapper deer prances with flair,
Wearing acorns like jewels in her hair.
"Nature's a ball!" she shouts with glee,
"Just look at that tree doing the cha-cha with me!"

The vines chortle as they intertwine,
Tickling the bark with a jokester's line.
"Why did the tree hide?" they all tease,
"Because it saw a squirrel with a penchant for cheese!"

Twilight comes, and toasting begins,
With all the creatures, their laughter spins.
Aubergine and gold, in funky style,
Dance through the night, trees rocking all the while!

Embroidery of the Emissaries

In the green where creatures conspire,
An emissary hedgehog sets the fire.
With spines all ablaze, he tells a jest,
"Watch out for that sleepy owl in his nest!"

Mice take the floor, with tap shoes of grass,
While ants shimmy by with a dash and a sass.
"Join our parade!" a bug shouts loud,
While caterpillars form a quirky crowd.

Twirling leaves whisper secrets to air,
A tapestry woven of joy and flair.
"Who needs a loom when you've got bright blooms?"
They stitch stories 'til the moonlight looms.

A chorus of chirps adds to the spree,
As crickets join in, filled with glee.
An embroidery of laughter, oh what a sight!
In this lively patch, all wrongs feel right!

Twine of Roots and Reeds

In the thicket, a rabbit hops,
Wearing a hat made of leaves, it pops!
A squirrel in sneakers, so cool and spry,
Chasing his acorn, oh my, oh my!

The mushrooms giggle, they're dancing awry,
While owls juggle twigs, and pinecones fly.
Beneath a bright moon, the critters unite,
To twirl through the night, what a hilarious sight!

A hedgehog in socks slides down a soft hill,
He rolls and he tumbles, with laughter and thrill.
The mice play a tune on an old wooden flute,
While frogs keep the beat in their best little boots.

So next time you wander where the wild things play,
Just look for the fun that's hiding away.
For beneath all the branches, the joy can be found,
In this silly realm of the creatures around!

Echoes of Bark and Blossom

An acorn debates with a seedling so small,
'Who's the best dancer?' they argue and sprawl.
The tree trunks sway, giving a nod of their bark,
While the leaves whistle tunes that are offbeat and stark.

Bumblebees plotting how to steal some grass,
While ants carry crumbs, oh, what a fine class!
Lizards in bowties, strut with a grin,
Competing for funniest, the chuckles begin.

A butterfly slips on a dew-dropped leaf,
And flutters away, but in comic relief,
Spiders spin yarns, a grand tapestry,
With laughter as threads, it's a sight to see!

So if you should happen to wander this way,
Join in the fun, let your worries all sway.
For even the blossoms, with giggles abound,
Are delightfully silly, where joy can be found!

The Seamstress of Sylvan Shades

In the glade, a rabbit tailors some clothes,
With fabric of petals, a new fashion grows.
A deer prances by, wearing trousers of moss,
While squirrels critique, and they giggle, emboss.

A hedgehog with needles fears pricking his nose,
As he stitches a shirt made of soft, fuzzy rose.
The frogs leap in tuxes, all ready to wed,
But end up in mud, oh, what a misread!

The threads of the spiders are used for a hat,
While owls debate 'Is that stylish or fat?'
The fox with a vest says, "I simply can't bear,
To walk down the runway with nary a hair!"

So come join the laughter, the creations so grand,
With critters designing, the wilds are their brand.
In this patchwork of giggles, where nature is free,
The seamstress of humor, you simply must see!

Shadows Tailored by Time

In shadows where whispers and giggles collide,
A raccoon with glasses and no place to hide.
He plans a grand party, with cake made of bark,
While pines crack up, with their comical spark.

The toads wear a tie, while they croak out their song,
And crickets in tuxedos, leap right along.
The wisps of the lanterns guide spirits with glee,
As they dance through the night, as wild as can be.

A badger with pencils draws smiles on his face,
While fireflies twirl, bringing light to the place.
The owls chuckle softly, and the stars join the fun,
As time stitches laughter, till the night comes undone.

So if ever you hear some giggles and cheer,
Just know there's a party, gathering near.
In the shadows of nature, where silly takes flight,
The echoes of laughter blend with the night!

Knots of Serenity and Growth

In a grove where squirrels dance,
Trees wear their mossy pants.
Twigs in hair, they're way too proud,
Chirps and giggles, oh so loud.

Leaves gossip like old friends,
Tickling branches that never end.
Bugs do a waltz, a silly sight,
As fireflies twinkle in the night.

Roots twist and turn like a rhyme,
Making paths that don't waste time.
Nature's jesters, frolic and play,
In this green laugh-fest every day.

Harmony in the Thicket

Chirpy birds in a wide array,
Start a choir at break of day.
Rabbits bop to the beat they find,
With a hop, hop, hop, unconfined.

Sticks act as drumsticks, tap-tap-tap,
Nature's rhythm, a cheeky clap.
A fox struts in, thinks he can sing,
But all he does is squeak and swing.

Frogs leap in with a croak so grand,
Mime artists of this woodland band.
Together they laugh, a melodic spree,
In their fun-filled ecological jamboree.

Tangles of Twilight and Dawn

As dusk creeps in, the frogs make bets,
On who can jump the highest yet.
Owls hoot, wearing glasses askew,
While silly raccoons paint their view.

The branches twist, a tangled game,
As shadows play tag without shame.
The moon joins in with a sparkling laugh,
While stars twirl in a cosmic half.

Glimmers of mischief greet the night,
As critters dance in pure delight.
Between the trees, tales start to bloom,
In the hush before the nighttime gloom.

Fabric of the Ancient Oak

An ancient oak with a crooked grin,
Hosts a chat about where it's been.
With knots and whirls, it tells a tale,
Of gusty winds that set it sail.

Squirrels clamber up its sturdy back,
Conducting treaties, snug as a wrack.
Acorns roll like marbles down,
As chipmunks wear the acorn crown.

The bark's a canvas, stories carved,
Of all the laughter it has starved.
In this wild realm of giggles and air,
Each branch provides a whimsical chair.

Mysteries Woven in Green

The squirrels play tag in the boughs,
With acorns as helmets, staking their vows.
A raccoon in pajamas, quite out of place,
Dances in rhythm with an awkward grace.

The trees whisper secrets, oh so absurd,
Like gossiping neighbors, they laugh without word.
A rabbit hops by, wearing a hat,
While the owl just chuckles, thinking how fat.

Down by the creek, a frog wears a crown,
He croaks out his dreams, with a hop and a frown.
His subjects, the fish, swim in disbelief,
Wishing for wings or a certain belief.

As shadows take shape in the dying light,
The critters join forces, plotting their flight.
In a world full of mischief, they frolic and play,
In this tapestry woven, they brighten the day.

Dreams Suspended Above

Up in the branches, a dreamer's delight,
A sloth on a swing, what a comical sight!
He snoozes so long, the sun's set and gone,
While the fireflies gather, their dance just begun.

An ant plays the banjo, with twigs for the strings,
Nearby, a bluebird tries on its bling.
The breeze carries laughter, the giggles collide,
With worms doing cartwheels, all filled with pride.

Clouds are the pillows for bunnies that nap,
While the fox holds a party, with snacks on the map.
The day drifts to twilight, as dreams take their flight,
In this merry abode, all is jovial and bright.

But wait! What is that? A raccoon with a hat,
Proclaiming a treasure, oh imagine that!
The laughter erupts, it continues till day,
In this whimsical haven, the fables will stay.

Tracings of Twilight Through the Trees

As twilight tiptoes with shoes made of gold,
A rabbit recites tales that never grow old.
He speaks of a turtle who raced with a hare,
But the winner was late, and nobody cares.

The shadows stretch long, embracing the ground,
While sing-songing crickets make whimsical sounds.
A hedgehog in socks, tapping under the moon,
Makes way for a night where the laughter's in tune.

The stars peek through leaves like a shy little child,
Each one with a wish, or a grin so wide.
The owls hoot their wisdom—so funny, so wise,
As possums play poker with acorns for prize.

When night blankets all with a quilt firm and fine,
Every creature joins in on this banquet divine.
Rustles of joy in the heart of the night,
With a sprinkle of laughter, all feels just right.

Melodies of Mossy Textures

A moss-covered rock is a throne for a sprite,
Bouncing with glee, in the pale moonlight.
With shoes made of leaves and a crown made of twine,
He throws a grand tea party, oh so divine!

The insects arrive, wearing fanciful hats,
And a snail brings the bread, placed down on the mats.
The air fills with giggles, a true merry affair,
As the mushrooms all dance, without any care.

An old toad croaks sonnets, with flair and with song,
While the beetles clap rhythm with legs—oh so strong.
In puddles reflect laughs that ripple and weave,
The tales of this gathering, too good to believe.

As night softly ends, with the dawn on its way,
They promise to meet for another fine day.
Where laughter and mischief belong to the trees,
In this joyous escapade, just a laugh in the breeze.

Harmonies in the Underbrush

In the thicket, squirrels dance and prance,
Chasing shadows in a playful trance.
Each bush a stage, each tree a seat,
With acorns dropping to the rhythm of their feet.

The rabbits gossip in a witty tone,
While a wise old owl sits all alone.
He rolls his eyes at the folksy cheer,
As hedgehogs giggle, 'Hey, the show's right here!'

Beneath the leaves, a chorus sings,
With frogs as tenors, and grasshoppers' swings.
The snorts and squeaks in a vibrant mix,
Nature's band leaves us in stitches, a great fix!

So join the fun, grab some moss for a seat,
As creatures collide in a playful beat.
Each rustle and murmur, a joyful affair,
Where laughter echoes through the wild air.

Sown in Silence and Solitude

In quiet glades where secrets lie,
A turtle tells tales, oh me, oh my!
'I've seen it all!' he boasts with pride,
While sneaky foxes just giggle and hide.

The mushrooms gossip and trade old news,
'Have you heard about the raccoon's new shoes?'
Beneath the ferns, a snail just shrugs,
'You call that style? I'd prefer a hug!'

A deer strolls by in a graceful panache,
With a cloak of leaves, it's quite the splash!
Yet one tiny mouse thinks it's all a show,
'Can we take selfies? You're way too slow!'

Amidst the quiet, laughter hides,
Every feathered friend throws off their prides.
Nature's whispers turn silly and loud,
In the stillness, they revel, each creature proud!

Weft of the Whispering Winds

The wind cracks jokes as it zips through trees,
Tickling the leaves, stirring up a tease.
'A gust of giggles here, a snicker there!'
A breeze prances by, flipping hair everywhere!

Amongst the pines, a trickster crow caws,
'Why did the squirrel climb? To grab applause!'
Each branch a stage for banter and jest,
In nature's comedy, they're truly blessed.

The chattering stream joins in on the game,
Splashing and laughing, never feeling tame.
'Catch me if you can!' the water purrs,
While fish flip and flop, narrating such slurs!

Echoes abound in this merry affair,
Where every sound is a chuckle laid bare.
The weft of laughter winds through the green,
In the joyous tapestry yet unseen!

Loom of the Woodland Spirits

In the light of dawn, sprites weave their tales,
Quirky and bright, they ride on the gales.
They dangle and dance, quite free in their flair,
Chasing the shadows without a care!

A bear in a tutu spins 'round a tree,
Muttering, 'Style's important, can't you see?'
The laughter of chipmunks, high on the logs,
As one tries to teach a tree to do yoga!

With twinkling eyes, the fireflies pop,
'Let's throw a party! Top the fun, don't stop!'
While the twilight hums a soft, silly tune,
As night drapes the woods like a whimsical moon.

Each nook and cranny a scene of delight,
Where spirits unwind in carefree light.
The loom of the woodland binds joy and surprise,
In the fabric of laughter, where whimsy lies!

Tapestry of Roots and Branches

In a dance of roots beneath the ground,
Worms tap ballet, making quite a sound.
Squirrels play tag with acorns galore,
While fungi chuckle at their crazy score.

The branches wiggle, a wild shimmy show,
With birds as the judges, they'll cheer and glow.
A raccoon wearing shades struts with finesse,
Declaring it's all just a furry mess!

Moss carpets giggle like they're hiding glee,
Flipping their fronds, oh, so mischievously.
The sap drips slowly, an artist's sweet flow,
Creating a masterpiece we'll never know.

In this tangled party, will you take a seat?
Join in the laughter, it's a rooty retreat!
With every twist, the joy multiplies,
In this merry chaos, no one ever sighs.

Echoes Among the Bark

Beneath the bark, there's a gossiping crew,
Trees whisper secrets that only they knew.
A woodpecker knocks, like a lawyer in court,
Claiming the sap's not just meant for the sport!

Beetles debate the best burrow to choose,
While ants argue over the tiniest clues.
A snail gets shushed, but takes it in stride,
He's just here for laughs, and a good moss ride.

All around echoes the laughter so grand,
The rustle of leaves gives a clap of its hand.
When branches all sway, it's a swaying ballet,
Fungi join in, with a fungal ballet!

So gather 'round closely, don't miss out the fun,
This bark-bound party has only begun.
With each little giggle, the forest is bright,
Turning dull moments into pure delight!

Loom of the Leafy Realm

In the loom of green, leaf threads intertwine,
A chameleon darts, claiming it's divine.
Spiders weave laughter in the shimmering dew,
Where dandelions dream that they're clouds, it's true!

Grasshoppers hop, wearing tiny top hats,
Debating who's faster, the dogs or the cats.
While fireflies blink as they gamble on light,
A game of who'll glow brightest in the night!

The daisies prance, lifting their little heads,
Wishing on wishbone dreams spun from threads.
With each story shared on a leaf's gentle sway,
The loom keeps spinning, come join the play!

In this leafy realm filled with thread and cheer,
Every little giggle you hear draws you near.
So grab a seat, let the fun be your guide,
In this woven wonder, let your laughter ride!

Canopy's Hidden Stitches

Up in the canopy, the stitches are sly,
As clouds act as pillows, floating gently by.
A clever old owl wears a monocle bright,
Critiquing the squirrels on their flighty delight.

The sunbeam stitches a quilt on the ground,
Where lizards play hide-and-seek all around.
When shadows grow long, they throw a big bash,
With critters all buzzing, oh what a flash!

A bear stumbles in, seeking honey's sweet fate,
He trips on a branch, oh the laughter is great!
Mice dance the tango, all squeaks and twirls,
In this high-up haven with chubby-cheeked squirrels.

With each little stitch, a new tale unfolds,
Of friendships and laughter in greens and golds.
So climb up the laughter, don't miss out, be bold,
Join the canopy party, let joy take hold!

Whispers of the Wild Weavings

Squirrels gossip in high trees,
While ants march on with ease.
Mushrooms wear hats, quite a sight,
Frogs croak jokes under the night.

Wolves howl with a comedic flair,
Bears dance, showing off their hair.
A raccoon's bandit act, oh dear,
Stealing snacks, then disappears!

Hummingbirds hum silly tunes,
Dancing with the fluffy plumes.
Each branch has secrets to share,
While creatures giggle everywhere.

The sun winks through leaves so bright,
Bouncing beams of pure delight.
With every rustle, chirp, and sway,
Nature plays in a funny way.

Echoes of the Timber Tides

Pine cones drop like comic bombs,
While beetles march in charming throngs.
Bamboo sways, whispering fun,
As critters scheme, a race begun.

Chipmunks chat, all fluffed with cheer,
Laughing at squirrels, 'Oh dear, oh dear!'
The brook giggles, making splashes,
While lizards strut in funny mustaches.

Trees whisper tales of their youth,
Some speak of love, some speak of truth.
But who knew that moods could change,
When branches sway, it all feels strange.

On a log, a raccoon sprawls wide,
Telling stories, full of pride.
Echoes of laughter fill the skies,
In this wood, surprise never dies.

Nature's Fabric of Life

Bees prance about on floral floors,
While butterflies act like tiny boars.
The owls wink in a cheeky way,
Making plans for a silly play.

Crickets chirp in a rhythmic beat,
While turtles shuffle on their feet.
Even the moss, so green and spry,
Cuddles rocks as people pass by.

A hedgehog dons a dandelion hat,
Hoping to charm a passing cat.
With each rustle, there's a jest,
In this realm, laughter's the best.

Raindrops giggle on the leaves,
Jokes that nature surely weaves.
Life here dances without a care,
Each furry friend gives laughter a share.

Threads of Leaves at Dusk

At twilight, the trees start to sway,
Whispering secrets in playful play.
The owls yawn, a bit overdue,
While fireflies flick and poke fun too.

A snail races—oh, what a sight!
With leaves for wings, he's ready to flight.
As shadows stretch and crickets chirp,
All around, the funny world lurks.

The wind carries tales from afar,
Of worms in a tatty old car.
Each leaf dances, a whimsical flight,
In nature's embrace, life feels just right.

As dusk drapes down in a silken gown,
All critters giggle, none wear a frown.
For in the twilight, full of glee,
The world spins round in pure comedy.

Nature's Emissaries in Twine

In a tangle of vines, a bird plays a prank,
Tripping up squirrels, oh what a clank!
The bugs start a dance, they waltz and they spin,
While ants throw a party, they invite all their kin.

A raccoon in pajamas, how stylish and bold,
Steals a snack from a picnic, oh, he's quite the mold!
With a wink and a grin, he munches away,
Leaving crumbs for the owls, who silently sway.

The mushrooms all giggle, they're tickled by flies,
As the sun starts to tickle, their laughter just flies!
"Let's hide from the rabbits, let's prank all the deer!"
Whispering secrets, they spread joy and cheer.

In this tangled-up place, where chortles abound,
The leaves flutter gently, creating a sound.
Nature's my stage, and life's full of quirks,
In the fabric of green, oh how humor lurks.

Delicate Layers of Time

In the morning light, a worm gives a shout,
"I'm the king of the soil, now watch me pout!"
And the grasses all giggle, they ripple with glee,
As the flies buzz around like they're hosting a spree.

The trees share their secrets in whispers of breeze,
"Did you hear what the owl said? I just can't believe!"
With roots intertwined, they keep passing the word,
"A squirrel's lost his acorn! It's totally absurd!"

A hedgehog rolls by, with a mischievous flair,
He tells all the hedges, "Guess who's got the hair?"
While flowers in bloom keep changing their hats,
Fashion shows for the bees, a catwalk for rats!

At dusk, the crickets play tunes oh so bright,
As the sun packs its bags, saying, "Time for the night!"
With laughter and joy, they count their dear stars,
In layers of time, we're all quirky avatars.

The Brush of Petals

Bumblebees gossip, they talk and they tease,
"Did you see that last flower? It's got quite a breeze!"
Dandelions tumble like fluffy balloons,
While ladybugs giggle to their own silly tunes.

A butterfly floated, in colors so grand,
"Look at my outfit! Isn't it just planned?"
But a moth swoops in, with a wink and a twist,
"Your glam's out of style; you should add a slight mist!"

Petals are painting the whole world in cheer,
Each hue a small answer: "Life is just dear!"
And raindrops, they chuckle, soaking the scene,
As plants form a conga, a fluid machine!

In this playful domain, where nature runs free,
It's a hoot when the grass gets all bendy with glee.
As petals blow kisses, oh what a delight,
In this brush of pure joy, everything feels right.

Shades of the Woodland Blend

The fox wears a scarf, it's quite the bold move,
With berries for buttons, he starts to groove!
Under logs, toads hop in synchrony grand,
While the ferns all salute with a wavy hand.

A raccoon with maracas shakes all through the night,
With fireflies joining, it's quite the sight!
The owls get confused and start hooting in time,
To the rhythm of nature, oh isn't it prime?

In shadows where laughter makes mischief arise,
The twilight joins in, painting laughs to the skies.
Dancing through leaves, the critters agree,
Life's lighter with mocks and jokes shared in spree!

Oh what a blend, where shades twist and twirl,
In a woodland that laughs, we all share a whirl.
With each tapestry woven, it's humor we send,
In the shade of the wild, let the fun never end!

Bathed in the Leaves' Embrace

A squirrel in a suit, doing a jig,
Dances with acorns, what a big gig!
The birds all laugh, they applaud with glee,
As he twirls and spins, oh, let it be me!

A deer with a crown, feels oh so spry,
Waging a battle with a butterfly.
They trade little jabs in a playful bout,
While the wise old owl just winks and shouts!

Beneath the great oak, a picnic is set,
With fruit-shaped hats, you'll never forget.
The ants in tuxedos serve lemonade,
As the sun casts shadows, they all serenade.

Today's the big play; it's opening night,
The raccoons are in, their masks fit just right.
With costumes of moss, they steal the scene,
In the laughter of leaves, life feels so serene.

Quiet Threads of the Night

Beneath the stars, a frog croaks a tune,
He dreamt he was dancing with a big balloon.
Crickets join in, they all tap their feet,
For a midnight concert, oh what a treat!

A hedgehog in glasses reads tales of the moon,
While nightcrawlers guide a parade in June.
With tiny bright lanterns, they light up the glen,
A gathering of critters, again and again.

A firefly whispers, "Check out my show,"
As he twirls and spins in a brilliant glow.
In the audience, laughter—each giggle a thrill,
Fluffy rabbits ruffle in a light-hearted chill.

As shadows grow long, the curtain must fall,
A bedtime for critters, the night calls them all.
Yet one bold raccoon shouts, "Meet here at dawn!"
For tomorrow's adventures, they'll all carry on!

Patterns in the Dappled Shade

Under a canopy, a raccoon draws nigh,
Wielding a paintbrush, with colors to try.
He splashes with flair, in hues bright and bold,
Creating wild patterns, a sight to behold!

Nearby, a rabbit prances in stripes,
Wearing a tie and preparing his gripes.
"Why can't we hop without making a mess?
All this fluff and fluffing is quite the distress!"

A wise old tortoise, with a cap on his head,
Takes notes of the chaos, he smiles instead.
"Art is a riot; it's all in good fun,
Just wait 'til the daisies decide to run!"

As the sun starts to set and the colors ignite,
Each critter shares laughter, delight in the night.
Creating their stories through whimsical play,
In the dappled shade, they'll forever stay.

Choreography of the Canopy Dancers

The squirrels take center, acrobatics on show,
With flips and with twists, they steal the tableau.
Above all the audience, this circus they make,
A tightrope of branches—their tails are at stake!

A wise old owl hoots, "Let's turn up the fun,
I'll add some wise beats, come dance everyone!"
The woodpecker drums with a tap-tap-tap,
As fawns join the fray, in a fanciful clap.

Fungi in tutus flit, spin, and twirl,
Spreading good vibes, giving life a whirl.
While ants in a conga line count to the beat,
Echoing laughter, a wondrous retreat.

So gather around and take part in the spree,
In the trees with their magic, they all feel so free.
With joy in their hearts and a giggle in mind,
The dance of the canopy, oh what a find!

Whispers of Woven Green

In the trees, the squirrels jest,
Chasing tails, they never rest.
Acorns fly like tiny ships,
Landing softly on my lips.

Mossy hats on toads they wear,
Dancing 'round without a care.
A rabbit winks, so sly and neat,
As I trip over my own feet.

Leaves gossip as the breezes sway,
Telling secrets of the day.
Branches sway in silly glee,
Tickling noses, just like me.

In this realm of woods and cheer,
Laughter echoes, far and near.
Nature's jesters, clad in green,
Making mischief, fit for a queen.

Threads of the Woodland Tapestry

Spiders spin their webs with flair,
Catching raindrops mid-air.
A deer prances, trying to dance,
While a frog sings, taking a chance.

Breezes tickle leaves above,
As birds croon songs of love.
Silly critters hop and play,
Turning mundane into a fray.

Mushrooms wear polka dot hats,
Holding parties for the rats.
Each twist of tree and vine,
Is woven laughter, oh so fine.

Squirrels compete in acorn races,
With grinning leaves as their bases.
In this patchwork of delight,
Nature's whimsy feels just right.

Loom of Leaves and Light

Sunlight dances on the ground,
While butterflies spin round and round.
A lumberjack takes a seat,
Leaning back, he's lost to defeat.

Woodpeckers drum a happy tune,
While critters plot beneath the moon.
A laughing raccoon with a snack,
Stealing treats, then off to pack.

Twigs and branches twist and tease,
Crafting art with perfect ease.
Nature stitches night and day,
In the most peculiar way.

Laughter weaves through every nook,
In this twisted, fun-filled book.
With every rustle, chirp, and cheer,
Nature's humor is always near.

Canopy's Embrace

In the treetops, giggles soar,
Bouncing off each leafy floor.
A chattering chipmunk, what a sight,
Plays hide and seek, from morn till night.

Branches jive with every breeze,
While ants march past with utmost ease.
Dandelions rock and sway,
They giggle softly, come what may.

Fungi throw a disco bash,
As mushrooms twirl and critters dash.
The sun peeks in with a sly grin,
Nature's jests are where we begin.

In this canopy, dreams unfold,
Each leaf tells stories bold.
With laughter stitched in every seam,
Nature lives the perfect dream.

www.ingramcontent.com/pod-product-compliance
Lightning Source LLC
Chambersburg PA
CBHW072139200426
43209CB00051B/171